GOAL FOR MEN

# WHAT IS YOUR 10 YEAR PLAN?

Clearly Define How You Want To Spent The Next Phase of Your Life

Patrick Newton

# Table of Contents

Chapter 1: How To Set Smart Goals ............................................................. 6
Chapter 2: Imporatnce of Goal Setting ........................................................ 9
Chapter 3: Commit to a Specific Goal......................................................... 13
Chapter 4: Reflect On Your Goals............................................................... 16
Chapter 5: Practicing Visualization For Your Goals ................................. 19
Chapter 6: Five Steps to Clarify Your Goals .............................................. 24
Chapter 7: Stop Setting The Wrong Goal................................................... 29
Chapter 8: Don't Wait Another Second To Live Your Dreams............... 32
Chapter 9: How To Stick To Your Goals When Life Gets Crazy ........ 37
Chapter 10: Becoming High Achievers ...................................................... 42
Chapter 11: Become A High Performer ..................................................... 47
Chapter 12: Changing How You Think....................................................... 51
Chapter 13: Becoming A Leader.................................................................. 55
Chapter 14: The Goal is Not The Point...................................................... 58
Chapter 15: Mastering One Thing At A Time........................................... 61
Chapter 16: Meditate to Rewrite Your Brain for Happiness .................. 64
Chapter 17: Successful People Start Before They Feel Ready................ 67
Chapter 18: How Smart Do You Have To Be Succeed............................ 70
Chapter 19: Three Skills That Will Pay Off Forever ............................... 73
Chapter 20: 7 Ways To Get Clear On What You Want To Achieve In Life................................................................................................................... 77
Chapter 21: 7 Simple Tricks To Improve Your Confidence.................... 82
Chapter 22: How To Rid Yourself of Distraction .................................... 86
Chapter 23: 8 Steps To Develop Beliefs That Will Drive You To Success ............................................................................................................ 90
Chapter 24: Get Rid of Worry and Focus On The Work........................ 96
Chapter 25: How To Stop Chasing New Goals All The Time ............ 100
Chapter 26: 6 Ways To Stop Procrastinating.......................................... 103

Chapter 27: Stay Focused ............................................................................ 107
Chapter 28: Focus – The Art of Alignment ............................................ 112
Chapter 29: Hitting Rock Bottom ............................................................ 114
Chapter 30: Positive Thinking For Men ................................................. 118

# Chapter 1:

# How To Set Smart Goals

Setting your goals can be a tough choice. It's all about putting your priorities in such a way that you know what comes first for you. It's imperative to be goal-oriented to set positive goals for your present and future. You should be aware of your criteria for setting your goals. Make sure your plan is attainable in a proper time frame to get a good set of goals to be achieved in your time. You would need hard work and a good mindset for setting goals. Few components can help a person reach their destination. Control what you choose because it will eternally impact your life.

To set a goal to your priority, you need to know what exactly you want. In other words, be specific. Be specific in what matters to you and your goal. Make sure that you know your fair share of details about your idea, and then start working on it once you have set your mind to it. Get a clear vision of what your goal is. Get a clear idea of your objective. It is essential to give a specification to your plan to set it according to your needs.

Make sure you measure your goals. As in, calculate the profit or loss. Measure the risks you are taking and the benefits you can gain from them. In simple words, you need to quantify your goals to know what order to set them into. It makes you visualize the amount of time it will take or the energy to reach the finish line. That way, you can calculate your goals and their details. You need to set your mind on the positive technical growth of your goal. That is an essential step to take to put yourself to the next goal as soon as possible.

If you get your hopes high from the start, it may be possible that you will meet with disappointment along the way. So, it would be best if you made sure that your goals are realistic and achievable. Make sure your goal is within reach. That is the reality check you need to force in your mind that is your goal even attainable? Just make sure it is, and everything will go as planned. It doesn't mean to set small goals. There is a difference between big goals and unrealistic goals. Make sure to limit your romantic goals, or else you will never be satisfied with your achievement.

Be very serious when setting your goals, especially if they are long-term goals. They can impact your life in one way or another. It depends on you how you take it. Make sure your goals are relevant. So, that you can gain real benefit from your goals. Have your fair share of profits from your hard work and make it count. Always remember why the goal matters to you. Once you get the fundamental idea of why you need this goal to be achieved, you can look onto a bigger picture in the frame. If it doesn't feel relevant, then there is no reason for you to continue working for. Leave it as it is if it doesn't give you what you applied for because it will only drain your energy and won't give you a satisfactory outcome.

Time is an essential thing to keep in focus when working toward your goals. You don't want to keep working on one thing for too long or too short. So, keep a deadline. Keep a limit on when to work on your goal. If it's worth it, give it your good timer, but if not, then don't even waste a second on it. They are just some factors to set your goals for a better future. These visionary goals will help you get through most of the achievements you want to get done with.

# Chapter 2:

# Importance Of Goal Setting

### Goals And Scores

Goals are targets set to be achieved. They are an important part of progress. In fact, your progress is measured by whether or not you have achieved your goals or if you are closer to them.

Maybe the term goal was coined from the soccer game rules. A team has to score a goal to win the match. Likewise, wins in life are measured by how many of your set goals you have achieved.

Everyone has goals. Families, society, and even the country. Without them, our progress is blind. But why is setting goals overrated?

It is overrated because the absence of goals is a recipe for failure. You will have nothing to look forward to.

Here are five major important reasons for setting goals:

## 1. Keeping You Focused

Goals will keep you on your toes. They will give you a reason to be on track with your projects. This is the reason why we set goals for ourselves or set standards for minors.

To some, the fear of failure is what keeps them on their toes. Failure is defined by the inability to meet set goals. This is clearly demonstrated in learning institutions. The school management, with the help of learners, comes up with a class target mean score annually. The idea is for one class to perform better than its predecessor.

The target will be achieved by the cumulative efforts of all stakeholders. Whenever issues come up at school, they will be reminded about their target mean score. Everybody resumes working towards the target.

That is the focus that goal setting inspires.

## 2. To Develop A Working Plan

It is said that a good plan is a job half done. When you have set a goal of achieving a certain target within a specified duration, what follows is developing a mechanism to make that possible. You cannot plan blindly.

A goal gives you a framework on how you can plan. There are many variables in meeting the target that will be unforeseen without a solid goal in place. In your plan, you can take care of what threatens the success of meeting your goal.

While still considering the example of goal setting in learning institutions, how do they work around meeting their target? It is after agreeing on the goal (target mean score) that they get to develop a working plan to achieve it.

A goal is a fundamental part of a working plan.

## 3. A Source Of Motivation

We draw our inspiration from our goals. In the first place, there is a reason why we set that goal. We were inspired to reach that particular level. The motivation to beat a mean score set by the last class of a national examination is what makes the next class set a higher target mean score.

The bar keeps moving higher with each successive examination lot. Goal-setting becomes a great source of motivation. We are continuously motivated by the desire to be better as measured by our goals.

Nothing should separate you from the sweet victory that lies ahead.

## 4. You Can Know When You Stray

Goals are like a destination. When you take a different route from where your destination is, you are definitely lost. Your distance and route from your destination determine when you will arrive if at all you will.

Goals help you to stay on track as you work towards achieving them. Without them, it is difficult to tell whether or not you are on the right track.

## 5. You Can Use Your Resources Optimally

There are always limited resources that we are likely to misuse when we are still guessing our way around life. This is all the more reason why we must figure out what we want to do with our lives and set personal goals for ourselves.

Goal setting allows you to use the available resources wisely. Everything will be for the greater good of the future.

The importance of goal setting cannot be overemphasized. These five reasons are enough reasons why you should consider it before it is too late.

# Chapter 3:

# Commit to a Specific Goal

A lot of us talk about what we are going to do. A lot of us have a lot on our to-do list that we are going to pursue or that we want to achieve. We all have ambitions, plans, goals, and dreams that we walk around telling everyone. But how many of us are actually doing something to achieve these goals?

The question we ask ourselves is that what are the things that we aspire to? What are the things that we want at no cost? What are the things that will bring us the ultimate happiness?

But none of us ask this; "What is the most important thing that I want to do today?".

The reality of this modern era is that we are busy with so many things that we don't have a clear image of anything anymore. Everything around us is going on and on and we are a slave to everything. Because we think that everything is equally important!

We want to have everything that the media showcases. We want all the glamour and all the success and every petty little thing. But none of us are actually getting any of that!

We need to have a discussion with ourselves once and for all; what is it that we are interested in, and what is it that we are committed to?

Let me clarify this a bit. You have a lot of things that you must do every day for a sustainable life cycle, but out of this daily grunt, what is that you are interested or curious to have, and what is it that must have at any cost?

I am sure you won't be able to come up with much! Because in life, not every stone is worth turning over. Not every tunnel is meant to be searched. Not every seed needs to be sown.
It's not bad to be curious about everything! Curiosity is what makes you set goals. But the reality is that you have one life and a small energy threshold. So why use it to gather everything? Why not put it all in just one basket at a time and let everything become somehow related to that?

If you are committed to a lot of things, you will try to master everything that doesn't even pair with any other thing. You will be distracted every hour of every day. Because you have put your eggs in so many baskets that you have lost count of the baskets.

But if you have one simple, yet important goal or dream, you will have a lot of time mastering a set of skills that complement each other at every step. This will not only increase your chances of getting to that goal but will also help minimize the time you need to reach that goal.

The less time it takes to achieve one, the more life you have ahead to plan and struggle for countless more goals.

# Chapter 4:

# Reflect On Your Goals

A good place to start is to look back at the short-term goals you set at the start of the year, as well as the longer-term goals you have for your career. Are you happy with the progress you've made so far towards achieving these goals? It's okay if you're struggling. Only 9% of people achieve their new year's resolutions, whether that's to get fit, kick a bad habit, or make real career progress.

While your goals may be clear in your mind, maintaining your progress is not always easy. How can you keep yourself on track? Here are some strategies to help.

## Try the SMART Technique

Ask yourself:

- is my goal Specific?
- is my goal Measurable?
- is my goal ultimately Achievable?
- is it Relevant to my values?
- is my goal Time-bound?

Using this method gives you clarity and detail on what your goal is and helps you track your progress toward it.

## Know Your Subgoals May Change

The subgoals you planned and the route to achieving your main goal may change along the way. That's okay – plans change. Don't be put off; it doesn't mean your end goal isn't achievable, it means you might need to take another path to get there. If you consistently miss your subgoals, consider a new route – or whether or not the end goal is still right for you and your career.

## Be Accountable

Hold yourself to account for achieving your goals by announcing them to others. Doing this also makes goals feel more 'real'. Start conversations about your goals with friends, peers or colleagues, so they can check in with your progress.

## Change Your Habits

If you find yourself stuck turning your goals into actions, try Moodnotes or the WOOP app (Wish, Outcome, Obstacle, Plan). Use these to form proactive goal-setting habits and observe your progress, so you can overcome barriers and stay on track.

## Be Aware of Your Edge Behaviours

An edge behaviour is an emotional, physical, or mental behaviour you experience as you come up against change, uncertainty or growth. An example of this could be procrastination or telling yourself you're not good enough. Being aware of how your behaviours shift is important because they impact your mood and your ability to move forward. Check in with your edge behaviours by recording, assessing and adjusting them so that you can adapt to change effectively.

## Track and Celebrate Your Successes

It's important to celebrate small wins because these incremental achievements help you stay excited about your goals. Every time you achieve something - no matter how small - write it down or make a note in your phone or planner. When you're feeling unmotivated, go through these previous successes to get perspective and boost your morale.

# Chapter 5:

# Practicing Visualization For Your Goals

Today we're going to talk about visualization and why I think all of you should practice some form of visualization every day to help keep you on track to the future that you can see yourself living in maybe 5 or 10 years down the road.

So before we begin today's video, i want you to write down some of the goals that you want to achieve. These goals need not be entirely monetary, it could also be finding a partner, having a kid, having lots of friends, playing in a tournament of some elite sport, playing fluent guitar, skateboarding like a pro, or even working at the Apple store maybe... any personal goals and dreams that you might think u want.

And In terms of monetary goals, it could be the kind of income level and the kinds of material possessions that you wish you had, for example a dream car of yours, a pretty landed house or apartment in a prestigious neighborhood, and nice flat screen Tv, a 10k diamond ring. Or whatever it may be. No matter how ridiculous, I want you to write these down.

Alright now that we have got this list in your hands, let's talk about what visualization is and how it can be a powerful tool to help you actually achieve your goals.

What visualization essentially is in a nutshell, is that it helps you step into the shoes of your future self, whether that may be 10 mins in the future, 10 years into the future, or even when you are at your death bed.

So why would we want to even think or imagine ourselves in the future when people have been telling us to be present and living in the moment etc. People including myself in my other videos. Well, you see, the difference is that with visualization, we are not looking into our past successes and failures as factors that influence our present state of mind, but rather to create a picture of a person that we want to be in the future that we can be proud of. A person that we think and aspire to become. Whether that be emulating an already rich or successful person, or simply just choosing to see yourself in possession of these things and people that you want in your life. Visualization can help us mentally prepare ourselves for our future and help us solidify and affirm the actions that we need to take right now at this very moment to get to that end point.

Visualization is such a powerful tool that when done correctly and consistency, our brain starts to blur the line between our present reality and our future self. And we are able to retrain and rewire our brain to function in the way that helps us achieve those goals by taking action more readily. If we have chosen to visualize ourselves as a pro tennis player, however far fetched it may seem, we have already decided on some level deep down that we are going to become that person no matter what it takes. And on a mental level, we have already committed to practicing the sport daily to achieve that outcome. If it is an income goal we hope to achieve, by visualizing the person we hope to become who earns maybe $100k a month, yes it might sound far fetched again, but it is certainly not impossible, we will take actions that are drastically different than what we are doing today to make that goal happen. A person who visualizes themselves making $100k a month will say and do things that are completely different from someone who tells themselves that they are okay to make just $2000 a month.

The action and effort taken is on a whole other level. A person who says they want to stay an amateur tennis player will do things differently than someone who visualizes themselves becoming the top player of the sport who is ready to win grand slams.

With these two examples in mind, now i want you to take that list that we have created at the start of the video, and i want you to now place yourself inside of your imagination, I want you to start picturing a future you that has already been there done that. A future you who has got everything that he ever wanted, friends, family, money, career, sports, hobbies, travel, seeing the world, all of it. And I want you to visualize how you actually got to that point. What were the actions that you took to get there? How much time did you have to spend on each activity each day, day in and day out, and the level of commitment and desire that you needed to have, the belief that you will and have achieved your wildest dreams, how that must have felt, the emotion associated with reaching your goals, and becoming the person that you've always known you could be.

As this is your first time, i want you to spend at least 5-10mins trying to see yourself in your future shoes. It might not come right away as even visualization takes practice. When we are so used to not using our imagination, it can be hard to reactivate that part of the brain. If you do not see it right now, I want you to keep going at it daily until that person in your head becomes clearer and clearer to you.

It might be easier to just see yourself as the next Warren Buffet, Jeff Bezos, Steve Jobs, Roger Federer, or whoever idol and superstar you wish to emulate. When you aim to emulate their success, you will mimic the actions that they take, and that could be a good way to start. Even a small change in your attitude and actions can go a long way.

Now that you have had a taste of the power of visualization, I want you to practice visualization on a daily basis. Again, everything boils down to consistency, and the more u practice seeing yourself as a successful person in life regularly, the more you believe that you can get there. Try your very best to pair that feeling with immense emotion. The feeling you get when you finally reached the summit. It will give you the best chance of success at actually following through with your goals and dreams.

To keep yourself motivated each day to practice visualization, click on this link and save it to your favourites of daily habits. Refer to meditation series.

This has been quite an interesting topic to make for me as I have used visualization myself with great success in helping me take consistent action, something that I struggle with daily, to reprogram my mind to work hard and stay the path.

# Chapter 6:

# Five Steps to Clarify Your Goals

Today, we're going to talk about how and why you should start clarifying your goals.

But first, let me ask you, why do you think setting clear goals is important?

Well, imagine yourself running at a really fast speed, but you don't know where you're going. You just keep running and running towards any direction without a destination in mind. What do you think will happen next? You'll be exhausted. But will you feel fulfilled? Not really. Why? Because despite running at breakneck speed and being busy, you have failed to identify an end point. Without it, you won't know how far or near you are to where you are supposed to be. The same analogy applies to how we live our lives. No matter how productive you are or how fast your pacing is, at the end the race, if you don't have clear goals, you will simply end up wondering what the whole point of running was in the first place. You might end up in a place that you didn't intend to be. Neglecting the things that are most important on you, while focusing on all the wrong things- and that is not the best way to live your life.

So, how can we change that? How can we clarify our goals so that we are sure that we are running the race we intended to all along?

## 1. Imagine The Ideal Version of Yourself

Try to picture the kind of person you want to be. The things you want to have. The people you want around you. The kind of life that your ideal self is living. How does your ideal self make small and big decisions? How does he or she perceive the world? Don't limit your imagination to what you think is pleasant and acceptable in society.

Fully integrate that ideal image of yourself into your subconscious mind and see yourself filling those shoes. That is the only way that you'll be able to see it as a real person.

Remember that the best version of yourself doesn't need to be perfect. But this is your future life so dream as big as you want, and genuinely believe that you'll be able to become that person someday in the near future.

## 2. Identify The Gap Between Your Ideal and Present Self

Take a hard look at your current situation now and ask yourself honesty: "How far am I away now from the person I know I need to become one day? What am I lacking at present that I am not doing or acting upon? Are there any areas that I can identify that I need to work on? Are there any new habits that I need to adopt to become that person?

Be unbiased in your self-assessment as that is the only way to give yourself a clear view of knowing exactly what you need to start working on today. Be brutally honest with your self-evaluation.

It is okay to be starting from scratch if that is where are at this point. Don't be afraid of the challenge, instead embrace and prepare yourself for the journey of a lifetime. It is way worse not knowing when and where to begin than starting from nothing at all.

## 3. Start Making Your Action Plan

Once you have successfully identified the gap between your present self and your ideal self, start to list down all the actions you need to take and the things that need to be done. Breakdown your action plan into milestones. Make it specific, measurable, and realistic. If your action plans don't work the way you think they will, don't be afraid to make new plans. Remember that your failed plans are just part of the whole journey so enjoy every moment of it. Don't be hard on yourself while you're in the process. You're a human and not a machine. Don't forget to rest and recharge from time to time.

You will be more inspired and will have more energy to go through your action plan if you are taking care of yourself at the same time.

## 4. Set A Timeline

Now that you have identified your overarching goal and objectives, set a period of time when you think it is reasonable for a certain milestone to be completed. You don't need to be so rigid with this timeline. Instead use it as sort of a guiding light. This guide is to serve as a reminder to provide a sense of urgency to work on your goals consistently. Don't beat yourself up unnecessarily if you do not meet your milestones as you have set up. Things change and problems do come up in our lives. As long as you keep going, you're perfectly fine.

Remember that it is not about how slow or how fast you get to your destination, it is about how you persevere to continue your journey.

## 5. Aim For Progress, Not Perfection

You are living in an imperfect world with an imperfect system. Things will never be perfect, but it doesn't mean that it will be less beautiful. While you're in the process of making new goals and working on them as you go along, always make room for mistakes and adjustments. You can plan as much as you want but life has its own way of doing things.
When unforeseen events take place, don't be afraid to make changes and adjustments, or start over if you must.
Even though things will not always go the way you want them to, you can still be in control of choosing how you'll move forward.

As humans, we never want to be stuck. We always want to be somewhere better. But sometimes, we get lost along the way. If we have a clear picture of where we want to be, no matter how many detours we encounter, we'll always find our way to get to our destination.

And you know what, sometimes those detours are what we exactly need to keep going through our journey.

# Chapter 7:

# Stop Setting The Wrong Goals

Setting the wrong goals will lead to disappointment in success.
Chances are you are aiming too low and
will not be satisfied with the outcome.
The outcome and the reason for
it must be clear before you begin.
Will the result make you satisfied?
Will you enjoy the journey to the result?
Your goal should encompass these questions
to make sure you are not setting the wrong goals.

You may be setting the wrong goals due to the expectations of others.
The goals you set should be personal to you -
something where you can enjoy the process and the result.
Is your goal likely to happen based on your current actions?
What could you do to make it more likely?
If you set the wrong goals, you will end up doing a whole lot of work you
don't like doing for a result you don't want.

Start at the end in your mind.
What would the end result look, taste and feel like?
With that you can imagine the process.

Can you do that work?

Would you enjoy that work?

Or would the reality fall short of your current expectations.

Life is chess not checkers.

The grand masters of success play 10 years ahead.

Thinking about how their actions today will

influence their lives ten years from now.

What's your 10-year goal?

What are your first steps?

Start at the end and work it back to now in your mind.

If you can envision the goal and paths to it

the battle is half won and you will have clarity over your goals.

Setting the wrong goals decreases your motivation to attain them.

You can only attain your motivation if your why is strong enough.

What are you aiming for and why?

If your clarity is strong enough, you will

feel the goal as if it is already real.

You can then confirm it is the right goal for you.

If you only feel half-hearted about something it is not for you

and it is probably a waste of your time.

It's better to go all out for something you really want

than to easily obtain something you don't.

The right goal for you will probably feel unrealistic at first.
People will probably tell you it is.
But you know that it really isn't.
If it's on your mind constantly then it
stands a good chance that it is the right goal for you.

You must think clearly about every aspect of your life
and the goal you wish to obtain.
Something that fits you and your true desires.

Your goal should be something that will make you happy as often as possible and give you the kind of financial life you want.
Never set goals because someone else thinks that is what you should be doing.
Only you know what you should be doing,
go after that and never accept anything less.
Gain clarity on your goals before you act.
Make sure it's something that will make you happy in the process and the results that come from it.

# Chapter 8:

# Don't Wait Another Second To Live Your Dreams

We often think we must be ready to act, but the truth is we will never be ready while we wait.

We only become ready by walking the path, and battles are seldom won in ideal circumstances.

Money is not the real currency in life, the real currency is time and every second we wait is a second, we waste.

Your biggest motivator is the ticking clock and the impending reality that one day it will be too late.

Your biggest fear is getting to 80 and realizing you haven't lived, that you haven't done what you wanted in life because of fear.

True regret is a medicine none of us want to taste.

We must decide what we really want, set the bar high, go after it now and accept nothing less.

You deserve respect, but you will live what you expect, this life will pay you any price but it's up to you what you accept.

You must act now from where we are with what we have, right now, not tomorrow or next week, right now.
Take the first step, make the draft plan.

Find out what knowledge you need to make this dream a reality.
Taking action now towards the goal in mind is crucial, if we wait, we risk losing the drive to make things happen.

We can never be fully ready because we don't know what exactly is going to happen, a lot of it is learned along the way - especially if you're doing something brand new.
If not, reading what has been done before in your area will give you a good understanding of what might work.

Every second we spend thinking about, instead of acting towards our goal is wasted time.
You cannot afford to wait because if you do not act, someone else will, someone else could also be thinking what you're thinking and act first.
Those who wait for opportunity will wait in vain because opportunity must be created, first in the mind, then in the world.

We cannot see the vast opportunity that surrounds us unless we believe it is there, believe it is possible and act on that belief, at the time it arises. The world is pliable, and opportunities do not wait for people to be ready. You must become ready on the road.

The obstacles you have to overcome on the move will mold you into the person you need to be to reach your biggest goals.

You must be patient, to be practitioners of who you believe you will be one day.

Getting into the mindset of whoever you want to be right now, because until you become that person in mind, you cannot in body.

As we start acting differently, different actions bring different results and if the new actions are positive and aimed at a certain goal, just like magic the world begins to transform for you, towards the life you wanted.

The leap of faith is acting now, feeling unready aiming for something that may seem unrealistic, but this is an essential leap and test to be overcome. As the days go on with the goal in mind, it will seem to become more likely, and you will feel more ready until it feels definite.

All things are possible but there will be required ingredients to your success you might not know yet, so the first step is to gain the knowledge required.

Once you begin to learn that knowledge you are on the road to your goal.

Organization and optimization of your time will make it easier to be efficient.

If time is the real currency, are you getting good value for what you spend your time doing?

If not, is it not time you used some of your seconds working towards something phenomenal?

You only have so many, and it is losing value every day as we age, think about it.

We must create a sense of urgency because it is urgent if you want to succeed in an ever changing world.

If we wait our ideas, products and services may become irrelevant because new technology and innovation is always changing.

Our ideas are only viable when they come,

Strike while the iron is hot is good advice,

When the ambition and goal is strongest and clearest.

Clarity is essential when pursuing dreams and goals, every detail of your dream should be clear in your mind down to the sights, colours and smells.

When we think about our goal, we should feel it as if it's already here, and start acting like it is.

Dress talk and walk as if you are that person now.

Whatever our current circumstances everyone has the ability to build in their minds, set the goal then determine the first step.

If your circumstances are bad there are more steps, but there are steps.

Start from step one and walk in confidence always keeping the big dream in mind knowing that this can happen for you.

We have a waking mind and a subconscious mind.

The subconscious knows things we don't, it is responsible for our gut instinct, which always seems to be right so follow that.

Everyday listening to that voice, keeping a clear vision of your goal in your mind and confidently taking action towards it.

It's possible for you if you act,

But time is ticking.

# Chapter 9:

# How To Stick To Your Goals When Life Gets Crazy

## Life Can Be Rocky

We all can agree that life can sometimes be noisy and messy. It can be chaos and madness and a single voice of reason in a room may lack. When life gets crazy, priorities change, and goalposts are sometimes shifted in the heat of the moment. Life is indiscriminate of your age or gender, and it can turn your goals upside down.

Sanity vanishes in thin air when life is marred by confusion. In this state, you will most likely replace your goals with others because they look more relevant and probably easily attainable.

Many people abandon 'fragile' goals when life gets bumpy. Some argue that a mouth-to-hand lifestyle is not ideal when chasing after your goals. Do not get mixed up in this confusion, retreat to sobriety and ask yourself whether you will do the blame game or work towards your goals. Be assertive with your rights elf.

## Get Your Priorities

Define your goals and how you intend to follow up on each one to completion. You cannot stick to vague goals. They have to be clear in your mind and the route to chase after them should be outlined awaiting execution. The common mistake most people commit is to say they will cross the bridge when they get there. This form of procrastination is misleading. Live the present and plan for the future.

A good plan is a job half done. Nothing should steal your focus from knowing your priorities. Not even the craze of life. Prioritize what is important and snob anything outside the plan no matter how lucrative or tempting it may present itself.

## Have Well-Founded Goals

The foundation of your goals matters the most in determining whether you will stick to them or not. Some people set unrealistic goals because of external influence and peer pressure. If you fall within this category, you will be chasing after an illusion and living a lie because your dreams are not in tandem with your personality.

Well-founded goals go beyond convenience. You set them based on your ability and vision of how you want to live your life. It should be devoid of exaggeration and imitation of the lifestyles of celebrities. You will be able to stick to your goals if you are true to yourself.

Authenticity and fidelity to the kind of person you will glue you to your goals. Is not that the dream you want to live?

Superfluous goals are changed from time to time for convenience. Question your commitment to your goals when you start shifting goalposts.

## Have A Thorough Understanding Of Your Environment

We are products of our environments. The role your environment plays in your life cannot be ignored. A toxic and unfriendly environment is incapable of manifesting your good goals. Instead, it will poison you to turn your back on the goals you had set. You may be a good person with pure intentions but your environment waters down all the gains you could achieve.

It is beneficial to exist in a good environment. It will channel positive energy your way to incubate your goals to their manifestation. Take time to understand your work or home environment and alienate yourself from any negative influence. It is better to be safe than sorry.

If circumstances demand, you can change your residence just to have a clear head to enable you to stick to your goals. Embrace positivity and watch yourself grow into the person you intend to be.

## Audit Your List of Friends

Have you ever heard of the saying that you are the average of your five friends? The impact of your friends on your life cannot be underscored. They, in cahoots with your environment, have the potential to ensure whether or not you stick to and realize your goals.

Sit down to rethink the type of people you consider to be your friends. If they are wayward, they will pull you away from your goals. They will want you to be like them and possibly make you abandon your goals if they do not align with theirs.

Your success in sticking to your goals even when life gets crazy is pegged on your choice of associates. Choose them carefully.

## Consume Inspirational and Motivational Content

Sometimes we need some positive energy in our lives to lift our spirits and soothe us that everything will be alright. Following your goals is a bumpy ride if there is nobody to encourage you. Read, listen and watch success stories to be encouraged.

Sticking to your goals is a conscious decision one makes and works towards it daily. You need a voice of reason to rise above that of discouragement. Finally, reason prevails, and you get encouraged even when at the brink of giving up.

In conclusion, it has become the norm for life to get crazy. Responsibilities bombard us right, left, and center. You need to be inseparable from your goals for you to achieve them.

# Chapter 10:

# Becoming High Achievers

By becoming high achievers, we become high off life, what better feeling is there than aiming for something you thought was unrealistic and then actually hitting that goal.

What better feeling is there than declaring we will do something against the perceived odds and then actually doing it.

To be a high achiever you must be a believer,

You must believe in yourself and believe that dream is possible for you.

It doesn't matter what anyone else thinks, as long as you believe,

To be a high achiever we must hunger to achieve.

To be an action taker.

Moving forward no matter what.

High achievers do not quit.

Keeping that vision in their minds eye until it becomes reality, no matter what.

Your biggest dream is protected by fear, loss and pain.

We must conquer all 3 of these impostors to walk through the door.

Not many do, most are still fighting fear and if they lose the battle, they quit.

Loss and pain are part of life.

Losses are hard on all of us.

Whether we lose possessions, whether we lose friends, whether we lose our jobs, or whether we lose family members.

Losing doesn't mean you have lost.

Losses are may be a tough pill to swallow, but they are essential because we cannot truly succeed until we fail.

We can't have the perfect relationship if we stay in a toxic one, and we can't have the life we desire until we make room by letting go of the old.

The 3 imposters that cause us so much terror are actually the first signs of our success.

So walk through fear in courage, look at loss as an eventual gain, and know that the pain is part of the game and without it you would be weak.

Becoming a high achiever requires a single-minded focus on your goal, full commitment and an unnatural amount of persistence and work.

We must define what high achievement means to us individually, set the bar high and accept nothing less.

The achievement should not be money as money is not our currency but a tool.

The real currency is time, and your result is the time you get to experience the world's places and products, so the result should always be that.

The holiday home, the fast car and the lifestyle of being healthy and wealthy, those are merely motivations to work towards. Like Carrots on a stick.

High achievement is individual to all of us, it means different things to each of us,

But if we are going to go for it, we might as well go all out for the life we want, should we not?

I don't think we beat the odds of 1 in 400 trillion to be born, just to settle for mediocrity, did we?

Being a high achiever is in your DNA, if you can beat the odds, you can beat anything.

It is all about self-belief and confidence, we must have the confidence to take the action required and often the risk.

Risk is difficult for people and it's a difficult tight rope to walk. The line between risk and recklessness is razor thin.

Taking risks feels unnatural, not surprisingly as we all grew up in a health and safety bubble with all advice pointing towards safe and secure ways. But the reward is often in the risk and sometimes a leap of blind faith is required. This is what stops most of us - the fear of the unknown.

The truth is the path to success is foggy and we can only ever see one step ahead, we have to imagine the result and know it's somewhere down this foggy path and keep moving forward with our new life in mind.

Know that we can make it but be aware that along the path we will be met by fear, loss, and pain and the bigger our goal the bigger these monsters will be.

The top achievers financially are fanatical about their work and often work 100+ hours per week.

Some often work day and night until a project is successful.

Being a high achiever requires giving more than what is expected, standing out for the high standard of your work because being known as number 1 in your field will pay you abundantly.

Being an innovator, thinking outside the box for better practices, creating superior products to your competition because quality is more rewarding than quantity.

Maximizing the quality of your products and services to give assurance to your customers that your company is the number 1 choice.

What can we do differently to bring a better result to the table and a better experience for our customers?

We must think about questions like that because change is inevitable and without thinking like that we get left behind, but if we keep asking that, we can successfully ride the wave of change straight to the beach of our desired results.

The route to your success is by making people happy because none of us can do anything alone, we must earn the money and to earn it we must make either our employers or employees and customers happy.

To engage in self-promotion and positive interaction with those around us, we must be polite and positive with everyone, even with our competition.

Because really the only competition is ourselves and that is all we should focus on.

Self-mastery, how can I do better than yesterday?

What can I do different today that will improve my circumstances for tomorrow?

Little changes add up to a big one.

The belief and persistence towards your desired results should be 100%, I will carry on until… is the right attitude.

We must declare to ourselves that we will do this, we don't yet know how but we know that we will.

Because high achievers like yourselves know that to make it you must endure and persist until you win.

High achievers have an unnatural grit and thick skin, often doing what others won't, putting in the extra hours when others don't.

After you endure loss and conquer pain, the sky is the limit, and high achievers never settle until they are finished.

# Chapter 11:

# Become A High Performer

We were put on this planet because we were meant to be all we could become. Human beings are the sum of their acts and achievements. But not everyone is capable of doing things to their full potential.

Every man's biggest burden is his or her unfulfilled potential.

So, what you need to become a high-performing individual in this modern era of competition is to idolize the best of the best.

You will need to understand the real-life features of a successful individual and what you need to do to become one.

If you want to be more successful in your life you need to become obsessive. Start your day with a goal and try your best to achieve it before you head to bed. You don't necessarily need to be on the right path with the first step, but you will find the best route once you have the undefeated will to find that path.

If you want to be more developed in your life you need to sleep effectively. The most successful people have a mantra of high performing routine. They don't sleep more than five hours a day and work seven days a week. They only take one day a week to sleep more just to rejuvenate their brains and body.

If you want to know if you are a high-performing successful person, look into your body language. If you find ease and leisure in everyday tasks, you are surely not standing up to your potential. If you like to sit for a conversation, start to stand. If you like to walk, start running. Get out of your comfort zone and start thinking and acting differently.

The last thing before you start your search for the right path to excellence is to set a goal every day. Increase your creativity by finding new ways to shorten the time of you becoming the better you and finally getting what you deserve.

You will eventually start seeing your life get on the track of productive learning and execution.

Change your way of treating others, especially those who are below you. If you are not a jolly person when you are broke, you can never be a jolly person when you are rich.

Never underestimate someone who is below you. You never know to whom the inspiration might take you. You have to consider the fact that life is ever-changing. Nothing ever stays the same. People never stay where they are for long.

It is the alternating nature of life that makes you keep fighting and pushing harder for better days. That is why you work hard on your skills to become a hearty human with the arms of steel.

Most people live a quiet life of desperation where they have a lot to give and a lot to say but can never get out of their cocoons.

But you are not every other person. You are the most unique soul god has created to excel at something no one has ever thought or seen before.

Start loving yourself. Stop finding faults in yourself. You are the best version of yourself, you just haven't found the right picture to look into it yet.

You want to be a high performer in every aspect of your life, here is my final advice for you.

If you push your limits in even the smallest tasks of your life, if you stretch your mind and imagination, if you can push the rules to your benefit, you might be the happiest and the most successful man humankind has ever seen.

Keep working for your dreams till the day you die. Life opens its doors to the people who knock on it. The purpose of this life is to knock on every door of opportunity and grasp that opportunity before anyone else steps forward.

You won't fulfill your desires till you make the desired effort, and that comes with a strong will and character. So, keep doing what you want to never have a regret.

# Chapter 12:

# Changing How You Think

## The Powerhouse Of The Body

Just like every car has an engine and mobile phones have batteries, so does the human body have the mind. It is the powerhouse of the body. Despite its small physical size, the power of the brain should not be underestimated.

The brain conceives an idea, considers its viability before it transforms it into an innovation. You are assured of a brighter future if you have a sober mind.

This vital function of the mind makes it a gem. It should be protected at all costs and well nurtured for the best results. Your thinking pattern is a result of the state of your mind.

## The Environment Factor

The environment affects the functioning of your brain, thinking, and reaction to many issues. Be wary of your environment. The performance of academically bright students can reduce when they change schools from high-ranking ones to lesser ones. This proven fact is evidence of the impact of the environment you are in.

What distinguishes the rich from the poor is how they think. The mind brings the difference in their lives. Once-upon-a-time friends can part ways based on their thinking habits. At some point, one even changes their residence. They no longer feel secure mingling with people whom they do not think alike.

## Thinking Patterns

There are divergent thinking patterns based on many factors. Apart from the environment, one's personality has a major role in determining how one thinks. Individual personality traits determine your shift in thinking behaviors.

Introverts and extroverts differ in thinking because of their different traits. One would take his time before deciding while another will decide at the moment. This does not make either of them right or wrong.

To successfully change how you think, you should first classify yourself correctly in the category you fall. If you are having a problem, consult a more experienced friend who shall be honest with you.

This is how you can change your thinking patterns based on your personality traits:

## 1. Social Exposure

Do you travel often? Or do you love making friendships with strangers? This is very important when you want to shift your thinking habits. While introverts enjoy their own company, extroverts love new experiences. They are outgoing and easily make new friends.

As an introvert, try being outgoing for some time. Make new friends apart from those you are comfortable with. This does not mean you should change your personality, but you should accommodate a different approach.

New friends will challenge your traditional thinking approach. They will inspire you to do things differently to obtain different results. However, be careful not to be carried away by popular opinion. Always seek to maintain your independence.

On the other hand, if you are extroverted, try minimizing external influence in your decisions. You are prone to thinking like your peers because you easily absorb new practices. Take some time to withdraw from the crowd. This retreat will make you see the blind spots that you cannot see when you are with your friends.

## 2. Education And Life Skills

Ignorance is the reason why many people make poor decisions. It is important to be enlightened because you will not fall into the traps that ensnare many. Education – formal, informal, or both – is light to our paths.

One thing about education is that we learn from the mistakes of other people instead of our own. When our turn comes, we can evade their mistakes. Through education, we walk in the footsteps of great people and become like them. Our thinking patterns can largely be influenced by our mentors.

Life skills sharpen our minds and teach us ways how we can face challenges. Although challenges mutate with time and become sophisticated, life skills help us to brave them. Do not despise life skills as part of informal learning, they are important in changing our initial perspective of things

In conclusion, changing how you think requires time to learn and effort to implement. It also needs a ready mind to try new things that will be impactful in their lives. Take the bold step today!

# Chapter 13:

# Becoming a Leader

Wow today we're going to talk about a topic that i think might not apply to everybody, but it is one that is definitely interesting as well and good for everyone to know if they someday aspire to be a leader of sorts.

Leadership is something that does not come naturally to everyone, while some are born leaders as they say, in reality most of us requires life experiences, training, and simply good people skills in order to be an effective leader that is respected.

To be a respected leader, you have to have excellent communication skills who come across as fair and just to your employees while also being able to make tough decisions when the time comes.

I believe that leaders are not born, but their power is earned. A person who has not had the opportunities to deal with others on a social and business level can never be able to make effective decisions that serves the well being of others. A leader in any organization is one that is able to command respect not by force but by implicit authority.

So what are some ways that you can acquire leadership skills if you feel that you lack experience in it? Well first of all I believe that putting yourself in more social and group settings in friendly situations is a good place to start. Instead of jumping right into a work project, you can start by organizing an activity where you are in charge. For example, those that involve team work and team games. Maybe an escape room, or even simply taking charge by organizing a party and planning an event where you become the host, and that usually means that you are in charge of getting things in order and all the nitty gritty stuff. Planning parties, coordinating people, time management, giving instructions, preparing materials... All these little pieces require leadership to pull off. And with these practices in events that will not affect your professional career, after you get a good feel of what it is like, you can move on to taking on a leadership role in projects at school or work. And hopefully over time all these practices will add up and you will be a much more holistic leader.

Soft skills are a key part to being an effective leader as well. Apart from professional expertise at the workplace. So, I encourage you to be as proficient in your learning of people skills and mastering interpersonal communication as well as being fluent in all the intricacies and details of your job description.

If you require a higher level of leadership training, I would encourage you to sign up for a course that would put you in much more challenging situations where you will be put to the test. This may be the push that you need to get you on your path to be the leader that you always thought that you could be.

Personally, I have always been a leader, not of a team, but of my own path. That instead of following in the footsteps of someone, or taking orders from bosses, I like to take charge of what I do with my time. And how to manage my career in that fashion. As much as I would like to tell myself that I am an effective leader, more often that not, I can honestly say I wish I was better. I wish i was better at managing my time, at managing my finances, at managing my work, and I have to always upgrade my leadership skills to ensure that I am effective in what I do. That I do not waste precious time.

Your leadership goals might be different from mine. Maybe you have an aspiration to be a head of a company, or division, or to lead a group in charitable work, or to be a leader of a travel tour group. Being a leader comes in all forms and shapes, and your soft skills can definitely by transferable in all areas.

So, I challenge you to take leadership seriously and to think of ways to improve your leadership skills by placing yourself in situations where you can fine tune every aspect of your personality when dealing with others. At the end of the day, how people perceive you may be the most important factor of all.

# Chapter 14:

# The Goal Is Not The Point

If you ever want to achieve your goals, stop thinking about them. I know this goes against everything anyone has ever said about achieving your goals.

Everyone says that think about one thing and then stick to it. Devote yourself to that one single goal as you are committed to your next breath. Check on your goals over and over again to see if you are still on track or not and you will get there sooner than you think.

What I am proposing is against all the theories that exist behind achieving your goals but wait a minute and listen to me.

The reason behind this opposing theory is that we spend more time concentrating on thinking and panning about our goals. Rather than actually doing something to achieve them.

We think about getting into college. Getting a bachelor's degree and then getting our Master's degree and so on. So that we can finally decide to appear for an interview that we have dreamed about or to start a business that we are crazy about.

But these are not the requirements for any of them to happen. You can get a degree in whatever discipline you want or not and can still opt for business. As far as job interviews are concerned, they are not looking for the most educated person for that post. But the most talented and experienced person that suits the role on hand.

So, we purposefully spend our life doing things that carry the least importance in actual to that goal.

What we should be doing is to get started with the simplest things and pile upon them as soon as possible. Because life is too short to keep thinking.

Thinking is the easiest way out of our miseries. Staying idol and fantasizing about things coming to reality is the lamest thing to do when you can actually go out and start discovering the opportunities that lie ahead of you.

Your goals are things that are out of your control. You might get them, you might not. But the actions, motivation, and the effort you put behind your goal make the goal a small thing when you actually grab it. Because then you look back and you feel proud of yourself for what you have achieved throughout the journey.

At the end of that journey, you feel happier and content with what you gained within yourself irrespective of the goal. Because you made yourself realize your true potential and your true purpose as an active human being.

Find purpose in the journey for you can't know for sure about what lies ahead. But what you do know is that you can do what you want to do to your own limits. When you come to realize your true potential, the original goal seems to fade away in the background. Because then your effort starts to appear in the foreground.

A goal isn't always meant to be achieved as it might not be good for you in the end or in some other circumstances. But the efforts behind these goals serve as something to look back on and be amazed at.

# Chapter 15:

# Mastering One Thing At A Time

I don't think anyone needs any explanation for the phrase, "Jack of all trades, Master of none". If you are one of those people who still can't get a grasp of this simple yet effective phenomenon, you seriously need to revisit your approach to life.

No one can be a true master. It's only a title for comparison. Mastering even one thing can be a task that can take decades. And once you become one, you can't guarantee you would remain the only person eligible for the title.

Yes, you would argue that you want to perfect everything because you want a better life and don't want any acknowledgment or applause. And I know it is well justified, but you need to focus on the bigger things.

Acknowledgment is important. It gives us the confidence to do more. But satisfying others for them to satisfy you is a stupid reason to pursue something. There is a lot of big fish out there for you to go and hunt.

You can go running around all day fetching small motives and goals, which would never profit you in the long run of life. Bigger chances always lie around us, but we are always too distracted to wait and get a good grasp of just one.

Instead of holding onto the one major thing, we cling to countless small ones and end up getting a little bit of everything. But we want everything and a lot of it, as our nature dictates us.

But the truth is simple yet harsh, "You can't always get what you want". You will never be able to get a hold of everything. But you can be good at just one thing and then try to make up the ladder with other singular things, goals, desires, wishes. And who knows, they might eventually get granted one by one.

We spend our life chasing so many things that we eventually get to a point where we are so exhausted that nothing encourages us, and we end up giving away all the hard work that we put in.

But life isn't always about giving up on everything else just for the sake of one thing. This misconception is common for everyone that if I go for one goal only, I might not get another chance for the others I had dreamt of.

You need to set your priorities straight. If you have a long-term goal, you need to go for the basics first and gradually climb up the ladder for the ultimate ideal for success.

But consistency and dedication are the traits that once you develop will always help you master everything that you ever come across till your last day on this planet.

Learn to say no to everything that gets in between you and your task at hand. Set your goals for the day and execute everything one by one. Don't leave anything half done, rather give every task your whole effort and your every new venture will see the dawn.

# Chapter 16:

# Meditate to Rewire Your Brain for Happiness

Suppose you've ever read the book Bridge to Terabithia (or seen the movie). In that case, you are familiar with Terabithia – an imaginary world that the main characters, Jesse and Leslie, create as a haven. It is somewhere they can go to be free from the cares and worries of the world.

Meditation has given me a Terabithia. I have created a clearing of calm and tranquility that I can enter into within seconds whenever I feel the need. I have a refuge no matter where I am or what I am doing. The worries of the world no longer threaten me. Except this mental place isn't imaginary, and it isn't populated with trolls and wild creatures – it is as real as the world we live in.

Since starting my meditation habit, my brain has been rewired for happiness, peace, and success. Here are just a few of the benefits:

I rarely become angry.

I find happiness in unexpected places.

I form deeper relationships and build friendships more easily.

However, by far, the largest benefit is that a deep, serene calm and peace is slowly permeating into every area of my life. At first, meditating felt unusual – like I was stepping out of normal life and doing something that most people find strange. I soon realized, however, that this wasn't true – millions of people meditate, and many successful people attribute part of their success to meditation.

Oprah Winfrey, Hugh Jackman, Richard Branson, Paul McCartney, Angelina Jolie... Any of these names sound familiar? All of these are famous meditators.

This list alone is powerful, but maybe you need a little more convincing that meditation is something you should try.

Michael Jordan, Kobe Bryant, Misty-May Trainor, and Derek Jeter are just a few successful athletes who rely on meditation to get them in the zone.

Rupert Murdoch, Russell Simons, and Arianna Huffington all practice meditation.

Arnold Schwarzenegger and Eva Mendez are just a couple more celebrities that make meditation a daily habit.

## Meditation Reduces Stress

Are you feeling the weight of the world on your shoulders? Meditation is incredibly effective at reducing stress and anxiety. One study found that mindfulness and Zen-type meditations significantly reduce stress when practiced over a period of three months. Another study revealed that meditation reduces the density of brain tissue associated with anxiety and worrying. If you want your stress levels to plummet, meditation may be the answer.

# Chapter 17:

# Successful People Start Before They Feel Ready

We all have humble beginnings. We all start from the womb of our mothers, living the same baby life everyone else has lived before us, and everyone after us will.

We get our lives as our parents serve them to us. They send us to get the education and sometimes we have to make those arrangements for ourselves. Sometimes we get the food hot and good-looking just being served to us without even wanting to ask for it.

But life isn't always this kind and caring.

How many times do we wish for things like I will do this better tomorrow, I will get that someday, I have to look for a better job, I have to do something about the extra weight that I am carrying.

We all have a wish list and it is always growing. But rarely do we do something about them. We always go back to our normal life and don't do anything about it as we always have. Sounds familiar?

It is the reality and the curse of living in this time of having everything we can wish so never wanting to struggle for other things.

There might be a lot of reasons for every one of us for not trying or trying but not getting what we want.

We lag in a lot of things and there are hundreds of explanations for them, but the most common is the 'FEAR'.

Fear of rejection, fear of waiting, fear of not being good enough, fear of the unknown, and mostly fear of starting something from scratch. All these fears are legitimate and justifiable, but you are not getting much by fear either. So why not be fearless and actually start doing something?

We have a lot on our plate, and we all have our bad days, but to start fresh, you don't need fear or an indicator or vision, you just need the tiniest of motivation that you have to make something for yourself and you and only you are your sole driving force.

Things will start happening for you one time or the other. You only need to maintain vigor at any age you are.

You don't have a set path. Don't think that you will get mature and stable once you hit the 30's or middle age. Time will not set the path for you. You, yourself have to set the time straight.

You don't need to be 30 to be mature, you can be 15 and still be a much mature and emotionally stable person than the one who has 5 children.

Your life is in your hands, and you have a responsibility towards yourself from the time you get a hold of your senses. Because you are always ready to turn things around.

You don't need to feel ready, but you need to show yourself that you were ready all along by just jumping into the pond of opportunities and the world will open its treasury for you.

You don't need to be perfect to start, but you need to start to be perfect!

# Chapter 18:

# How Smart Do You Have To Be To Succeed

How smart do you have to be to succeed? How intelligent do you need to be to become a successful entrepreneur? How well does your training program need to be to become an elite athlete? How perfect does your weight loss program need to be to burn fat?

We don't often ask ourselves questions, but they are built into our beliefs and actions about many phases of life. We often think that we aren't succeeding because we haven't found the right strategy or because we weren't born with the right talents. Perhaps that is true. Or, perhaps there is an untold side of the story.

## Threshold Theory

The surprising discovery that came out of Terman's study is best described by creativity researcher and physician Nancy Andreasen as Threshold Theory…

*"Although many people continue to equate intelligence with genius, a crucial conclusion from Terman's study is that having a high IQ is not equivalent to being highly creative.*

*Subsequent studies by other researchers have reinforced Terman's conclusions, leading to what's known as the threshold theory, which holds that above a certain level, intelligence doesn't have much effect on creativity: most creative people are pretty smart, but they don't have to be that smart, at least as measured by conventional intelligence tests. An IQ of 120, indicating that someone is very smart but not exceptionally so, is generally considered sufficient for creative genius."*

## Threshold Theory In Everyday Life

If you look around, you'll see that the Threshold Theory applies to many things in life. There is a minimum threshold of competence that you need to develop in nearly any endeavor. Success is rarely as simple as "just work harder."

Beyond that threshold, however, the difference is between those who put in the work and those who get distracted. Once you have a basic grasp of the right things to do, it becomes about the consistency of doing the right things more often. Once you understand the fundamentals, it comes down to your habits.

# Writing

Assuming you understand the core principles of writing and the basics of grammar, what determines your ability to write well more than anything else is writing a lot. Once you reach the threshold of writing a decent sentence, the thing that leads to success is writing more.

# Entrepreneurship

Assuming you know what the most important metric is for your business, what makes the biggest difference is focusing on that metric every day. Once you cross the basic threshold of knowing what to work on, the most important thing is continuing to work on that one thing and not something else.

If you're brand new to an area, then it's possible you haven't learned enough to cross the threshold yet. But for most of us, we know what works, and we have enough knowledge to make progress. It's not about being more intelligent or more skilled, and it's about overcoming distraction and doing the work that already works.

# Chapter 19:

# Three Skills That Will Pay Off Forever

The world is changing all the time. There are new technologies every day, companies come and go, and most methods we use to achieve something are no longer practical. That made me think at one point, "what skills should I learn to be better than the rest?" or better, "what abilities should I learn, that could pay off forever?"

There are already many people doing what you are doing right now, and even better than you. The key is a proven system and a series of abilities that makes what you do stand out from the mass, even if you are not the best.

Here are three valuable skills to master now that will pay off forever in your business and professional area and will help your knowledge make an impact from the rest.

# 1. Shift Your Mind from Job Economy To Entrepreneur Economy

Not everyone wants to be a full-time entrepreneur. I personally have a full-time job for now.

However, there is a difference between the mentality of a person who has been an employee all his life and one who creates a business and learning that could help you achieve anything you want in life. For example, even though I have a full-time job, I negotiated with my boss to work at my pace and by deliverables instead of the hour. This way, I control my time and what I do while maintaining good work status. I am also always looking for ways to delegate tasks and automate manual processes.

Another way this skill helped me is to find solutions and business opportunities where others see problems in my work area. For example, many people complained about having the same task every day because many clients started asking for them, and it was very manual and lengthy. Instead of complaining, I created a software application that solves that situation, and now I just have to click two buttons to solve this issue.

An entrepreneur economy mindset is a valuable skill that will pay off forever because it will help you find opportunities, negotiate your work schedule and environment, know where and how to invest, and manage a side hustle.

## 2. Be An Engaging Person

Communication is important. But it doesn't matter how good you are speaking if people don't engage with what you are saying. If you can't engage your audience and make them excited to hear what you have to say, you will struggle to get them to absorb your message or buy anything from you.

The best way to develop this skill is to have passion for what you do. When you talk about things you love, you act and speak differently, like when you don't care about something. So make sure to be confident of what you do and sell.

This skill has helped me get clients and job opportunities because I learned how people could connect with me and the story I'm telling, even if it's only telling them why I chose my career. The ability to overcome your emotions to keep working on your goals

I think the toughest thing about adulthood is that your life could be crumbling, and you still have to show up and do what you need to do.

While emotions can have a beneficial role in your life, they can take a toll on your emotional health and relationships when they get out of control. So, one skill that will help you on any ambit of your life is the ability to overcome your emotions so you can keep working even if you are not in a good mood.

One way to start growing this skill is to work with a system instead of by motivation. When you work only by motivation, you will not be able to advance every day, but when you do it with a system, it doesn't matter how you wake up; you fulfill your routine.

## 3. The Ability to Break A Process Down Into Smaller Steps

One of the reasons I've given up on so many projects is because of how overwhelming they look when I'm starting out. The problem with this is that we see a goal as a single process, and we feel that it is too big that we cannot achieve it.

Goals like "Be fit," "learn a new language," "create a successful business," or "write a book" are processes too general and big, so when you try to achieve them, it looks practically impossible. Breaking processes into smaller steps helped me achieve those big goals in small daily habits that I can include in my routine.

# Chapter 20:

# 7 Ways to Get Clear On What You Want To Achieve In Life

Over time, you might be wondering what makes a person successful and why some people achieve success easier than others? The answer may differ from person to person, but it is a lot more than just setting a goal. As we become clear on our definition of success, it usually changes our perspective on life. With different insights such as these, our goal becomes more directive, and our achievement and motivation levels increase.

Here are 7 Ways to Get Clarity:

## 1. Success and Mindset Go Hand In Hand

The first and foremost tip of becoming successful is to know what success means for you. When you identify this, you will be directed towards your objective or goal, making it easier to achieve it. The second part is your mindset, as it plays a massive role in your success. You might notice that although you might be doing the same thing as hundreds of others, you still aren't getting anywhere. Therefore, you should develop a success mindset instead of being frustrated with it. Below are some ways to help you get clear on what you want to achieve in your life and develop a success mindset.

## 2. Be Clear on Your Version of Success

Gaining clarity will positively affect your mindset, and it's vital to being and feeling successful. We might know what success means to us in our unconscious mind, but we aren't precisely implementing it in our everyday life. This can make it challenging to access our truth. The need to communicate with ourselves honestly and find some answers arises in such situations. We need to sit somewhere quiet, meditate, and ask ourselves about what we want in life. The answers might not come straight away, but it is essential to know your version of success and what you associate with it.

## 3. Stretch Yourself

When setting our goals, it's crucial to step out of our comfort zone and include a few elements that will help us stretch and grow to achieve those goals. These might be doing something that you are usually not comfortable with or afraid of doing, such as public speaking, or simply learning a new skill that doesn't come easy on you. By doing this, you will help set a breakthrough goal that would represent a quantum leap. Examples of breakthrough goals include publishing a book, starting a business, or quitting your current job to get a new one. Of course, material goals are essential, but it all comes down to becoming a life master. The most significant benefit we receive while pursuing our dreams is who we become in the process. As motivational philosopher Jim Rohn advises, "You should set a goal big enough that in the process of achieving it, you become someone worth becoming."

## 4. Work on Your Goals Daily

Please make a list of all your goals and go through them every day to make sure your subconscious mind is focused on what you want. No matter how slow or small, your progress is, it counts as long as you decide not to give up and keep going. As the old joke runs, "How do you eat an elephant? One bite at a time." Similarly, steady progress in bite-sized chunks will eventually put the huge goals into reach. Thus, success isn't a one-time thing, but rather it is a system of gradual efforts.

## 5. Your Goals Should Impact Others

There's not a single person on this earth who can say that he got successful on his own, without any help from anyone. The truth is, we always need a helping hand in the process of becoming something. As soon as we commit to big dreams and goals and go after them, our subconscious mind comes up with big creative ideas to make all of them happen. Then, we will start attracting the people, opportunities, and resources that we need to make our dreams come true. Big dreams not only inspire us but also compel others to play a bit too. When you discover that accomplishing something just isn't for you but also contributing to the betterment of others, it will accelerate the accomplishment of the goal.

## 6. Reflect and Readjust Without Beating Yourself Up

Reflection is one of the most critical success tips, yet it is one of the most crucial elements often ignored or forgotten to rush to the finishing line. For each action that we take, we must be aware of whether it worked or not and then be prepared to change what we are doing until we achieve the outcome. Reflection helps us with all of this. It's ineffective if we just run full steam ahead blindly without pausing for a progress check. It is also important to be kind with yourself when reflecting, as beating yourself up will do no good to you. On the contrary, it will lower your self-esteem and makes it difficult for you to work up to your full potential.

## 7. Take Good Care of Your Mind and Body

Our mind and body play a vital role in how successful we become. Therefore, it is crucial to adopt the physiology and psychology of excellence. We must understand that our mind can impact our physical health and our body, too, has an enormous effect on our emotional state. If we feel low in energy and have negative thoughts, it can immensely affect how we perform our daily activities. Nurture your mind, body, and soul, your performance will excel, and you will experience more successful outcomes.

## Conclusion

Take a set of rules on what and how you want to achieve things in your life. Implement them daily and consistently, and you will begin to know what's important to you, which will give you a solid foundation to develop a clear mindset and achieve your goals.

# Chapter 21:

# 7 Simple Tricks To Improve Your Confidence

So many successful people acclaim their self-esteem and confidence for their success. But few people explain how to build confidence or how to become confident. It's hard because confidence is built on different things, but it's built on choices and achievements that fuel your passions and make you happy and proud of who you are. Exploring these is one of the most enjoyable activities of your life. Here are a few ways to start building your confidence:

## 1. Get Things Done

Confidence is built on achievement. If you achieve significant and small goals, you will feel much better. It starts with your daily goal. What do you need to accomplish today and every day of this week or three days this week to help you reach your goal? If you hit the goals you've set for yourself every day, you'll most likely start to hit weekly and monthly goals, bringing you closer to your semi-annual and annual goal ranges. Remember that progress is incremental, and significant changes don't happen overnight. You will feel like you can take on a big project and set yourself a lofty goal because you think you can achieve it. Set a goal and do it.

## 2. Monitor Your Progress

The best way to achieve your goals, big or small, is to break them down into smaller goals and track your progress. Whether you're trying to get a promotion, get a better job, go to college, change careers, eat healthier, or lose 10 pounds, the best way to know if you're making progress is to follow them. Try to quantify your accomplishments: how many job applications you apply for or go to college, what you eat and how much you exercise; write down any of your goals. It will keep you on track, and you will gain confidence in seeing your progress in real-time.

## 3. Do The Right Thing

The most confident people live by a value system and make decisions based on it, even when it's difficult and not necessarily in their best interest but in the greater good. Your actions and decisions define your personality. Ask yourself what the best version of yourself you would like to be and do it. Even if it's tough and it's the last thing you want to do, and it means a short-term sacrifice on your part, in the long run, you'll love yourself more and be more proud of who you are.

## 4. Exercise

In addition to benefiting your overall health, exercise helps maintain memory, improves concentration, helps manage stress, and prevents depression. It's hard to worry when you don't have excess energy to absorb, and besides being uncomfortable at times, exercise improves all aspects of your life. So stay active and make time to take care of yourself.

## 5. Be Fearless

Failure is not your enemy, and it is the fear of failure that paralyzes you. If you set big goals and dream big, you will feel overwhelmed and confident that you cannot achieve them. In times like these, you have to look inside yourself, gather every bit of courage you have, and keep going. All wildly successful people are afraid, and they keep working and taking risks because what they're trying to accomplish is more important and urgent than the fear of failure. Think about how much you want to achieve your goal, then put your worry aside and move on, one day at a time.

## 6. Follow Through

People respect people when they say they will do something, and they will do it. More importantly, you'll respect yourself if you say you'll do something and do it, and confidence will come more manageable because you know you don't mind the hard work. Actions give meaning to your words and will help pave the way for you to achieve your goals, strengthen relationships, and feel proud of who you are.

## 7. Do More of What Makes You Happy

What do you like to do in your spare time? Is it for hiking, kayaking, and enjoying the outdoors? Or do you live to lie on your sofa and watch all the great television available? Whatever you love, make space for it because life is short; you need time to enrich your life and rejuvenate yourself to be your best self.

# Chapter 22:

# How To Rid Yourself of Distraction

Distraction and disaster sound rather similar.
It is a worldwide disorder that you are probably suffering from.
Distraction is robbing you of precious time during the day.
Distraction is robbing you of time that you should be working on your goals.
If you don't rid yourself of distraction, you are in big trouble.

It is a phenomenon that most employees are only productive 3 out of 8 hours at the office.
If you could half your distractions, you could double your productivity.
How far are you willing to go to combat distraction?
How badly do you want to achieve proper time management?

If you know you only have an hour a day to work, would it help keep you focused?

Always focus on your initial reason for doing work in the first place.
After all that reason is still there until you reach your goal.

Create a schedule for your day to keep you from getting distracted.
Distractions are everywhere.
It pops up on your phone.
It pops up from people wanting to chat at work.
It pops up in the form of personal problems.
Whatever it may be, distractions are abound.

The only cure is clear concentration.
To have clear concentration it must be something you are excited about.
To have clear knowledge that this action will lead you to something exciting.

If you find the work boring, it will be difficult for you to concentrate too long.
Sometimes it takes reassessing your life and admitting your work is boring for you to consider a change in direction.

Your goal will have more than one path.
Some paths boring, some paths dangerous, some paths redundant, and some paths magical.
You may not know better until you try.
After all the journey is everything.

If reaching your goal takes decades of work that makes you miserable, is it really worth it?
The changes to your personality may be irreversible.

Always keep the goal in mind whilst searching for an enjoyable path to attain it.
After all, if you are easily distracted from your goal, then do you really want it?

Ask yourself the hard questions.
Is this something you really want? Or is this something society wants for you?

Many people who appear successful to society are secretly miserable.
Make sure you are aware of every little detail of your life.
Sit down and really decide what will make you happy at the end of your life.

What work will you be really happy to do?
What are the causes and people you would be happy to serve?
How much money you want?
What kind of relationships you want?
If you can build a clear vision of this life for you, distractions will become irrelevant.
Irrelevant because nothing will be able to distract you from your perfect vision.

Is what you are doing right now moving you towards that life?
If not stop and start doing the things what will.
It really is that simple.

Anyone who is distracted for too long from the task in hand has no business doing that task. They should instead be doing something that makes them happy.

We can't be happy all the time otherwise we wouldn't be able to recognize it.
But distraction is a clear indicator you may not be on the right path for you.
Clearly define your path and distraction will be powerless.

# Chapter 23:

# 8 Steps To Develop Beliefs That Will Drive you To Success

'Success' is a broad term. There is no universal definition of success, it varies from person to person considering their overall circumstances. We can all more or less agree that confidence plays a key role in it, and confidence comes from belief.

Even our most minute decisions and choices in life are a result of believing in some specific outcome that we have not observed yet.

However, merely believing in an ultimate success will not bring fortune knocking at your door. But it certainly can get you started—take tiny steps that might lead you towards your goal. Now, since we agree that having faith can move you towards success, let's look at some ways to rewire your brain into adopting productive beliefs.

Here are 8 Steps to Develop Beliefs That Will Drive You To Success:

## 1. Come Up With A Goal

Before you start, you need to decide what you want to achieve first. Keep in mind that you don't have to come up with something very specific right away because your expectations and decisions might change over time. Just outline a crude sense of what 'Achievement' and 'Success' mean to you in the present moment.

Begin here. Begin now. Work towards getting there.

## 2.  Put Your Imagination Into Top Gear

"Logic will take you from A to B. Imagination will take you everywhere", said Albert Einstein.

Imagination is really important in any scenario whatsoever. It is what makes us humans different from animals. It is what gives us a reason to move forward—it gives us hope. And from that hope, we develop the will to do things we have never done before.

After going through the first step of determining your goal, you must now imagine yourself being successful in the near future. You have to literally picture yourself in the future, enjoying your essence of fulfilment as vividly as you can. This way, your ultimate success will appear a lot closer and realistic.

## 3. Write Notes To Yourself

Writing down your thoughts on paper is an effective way to get those thoughts stuck in your head for a long time. This is why children are encouraged to write down what is written in the books instead of memorizing them just by reading. You have to write short, simple, motivating notes to yourself that will encourage you to take actions towards your success. It doesn't matter whether you write in a notebook, or on your phone or wherever—just write it. On top of that, occasionally read what you've written and thus, you will remain charged with motivation at all times.

## 4. Make Reading A Habit

There are countless books written by successful people just so that they can share the struggle and experience behind their greatest achievements. In such an abundance of manuscripts, you may easily find books that portray narratives similar to your life and circumstances. Get reading and expand your knowledge. You'll get never-thought-before ideas that will guide you through your path to success. Reading such books will tremendously strengthen your faith in yourself, and in your success. Read what other successful people believed in—what drove them. You might even find newer beliefs to hold on to. No wonder why books are called 'Man's best friend'.

## 5. Talk To People Who Motivates You

Before taking this step, you have to be very careful about who you talk to. Basically, you have to speak out your goals and ambitions in life to someone who will be extremely supportive of you. Just talk to them about what you want, share your beliefs and they will motivate you from time to time towards success. They will act as powerful reminders. Being social beings, no human can ever reject the gist of motivation coming from another human being—especially when that is someone whom you can rely on comfortably. Humans have been the sole supporter of each other since eternity.

## 6. Make A Mantra

Self-affirming one-liners like 'I can do it', 'Nothing can stop me', 'Success is mine' etc. will establish a sense of firm confidence in your subconscious mind. Experts have been speculative about the power of our subconscious mind for long. The extent of what it can do is still beyond our grasp. But nonetheless, reciting subtle mantras isn't a difficult task.

Do it a couple of times every day and it will remain in your mind for ages, without you giving any conscious thought to it. Such subconscious affirmations may light you up in the right moment and show you the path to success when you least expect it.

## 7. Reward Yourself From Time To Time

Sometimes, your goals might be too far-fetched and as a result, you'll find it harder to believe in something so improbable right now. In a situation like this, what you can do is make short term objectives that ultimately lead to your main goal and for each of those objectives achieved, treat yourself with a reward of any sort—absolutely anything that pleases you. This way, your far cry success will become more apparent to you in the present time. Instant rewards like these will also keep you motivated and make you long for more. This will drive you to believe that you are getting there, you are getting closer and closer to success.

## 8. Having Faith In Yourself

Your faith is in your hands alone. How strongly you believe in what you deserve will motivate you. It will steer the way for self-confidence to fulfill your inner self. You may be extremely good at something but due to the lack of faith in your own capabilities, you never attempted it—how will you ever know that you were good at that? Your faith in yourself and your destined success will materialize before you through these rewards that you reserve for yourself. You absolutely deserve this!

## Final Thoughts

That self-confidence and belief and yourself, in your capabilities and strengths will make you work towards your goal. Keep in mind that whatever you believe in is what you live for. At the end of the day, each of us believed in something that made us thrive, made us work and move forward. Some believed in the military, some believed in maths, some believed in thievery—everyone had a belief which gave them a purpose—the purpose of materializing their belief in this world. How strongly you hold onto your belief will decide how successful you will become.

# Chapter 24:

# Get Rid of Worry and Focus On The Work

Worry is the active process of bringing one's fears into reality.
Worrying about problems halts productivity by taking your mind off the work in hand.
If you're not careful, a chronic state of worrying can lead you down a dark path that you might find hard to get out of.

Always focus on the required work and required action towards your dream.
Anything could happen, good or bad,
but if you remain focused and do the work despite the problems,
you will through with persistence and succeed.

Always keep your mind on the goal,
your eyes on the prize.
Have an unwavering faith in your abilities no matter what.

Plan for the obvious obstacles that could stand in your way,
but never worry about them until you have to face them.
Tackle it with confidence as they come and move forward with pride.

Problems are bound to arise.

Respond to them necessarily along the way if they actually happen.

After all, most worries never make it into reality.

Instead focus on what could go right.

Focus on how you can create an environment that will improve your chances of success.

You have the power over your own life and direction.

As children we dreamed big.

We didn't think about all the things that could go wrong.

As children we only saw the possibilities.

We were persistent in getting what we wanted no matter the cost.

As adults we need to be reminded of that child-like faith.

To crush worry as if it were never there.

To only focus on the possibilities.

You cannot be positive and negative at the same time.

You cannot be worrying and hopeful of the future.

You cannot visualize your perfect life while worrying about everything that could go wrong.

Choose one.

Stick to it.

Choose to concentrate on the work.

The result will take care of your worries.

Catch yourself when you feel yourself beginning to worry about things. Instead of dwelling on the problem, choose to double down on the action.
Stay focused and steadfast in the vision of your ultimate goal.

The work now that you must do is the stepping stones to your success.
The work now must have your immediate attention.
The work now requires you to cast worry aside in favour of concentration and focus.

How many stepping stones are you away?
What is next?
Push yourself every single day.
Because only you have the power to create your future.
If not, things will remain the same as they have always been.

Always have a clearly defined goal,
A strong measure of faith,
And an equally strong measure of persistence and grit.
These are the ingredients to creating the life you want.
A life of lasting happiness and success.

Take control instead of accepting things as they are.
Reject anything else that is not the goal that you've set for yourself.
Whatever goal you set, ten times it, and focus on it every day.
The focus will keep your mind on the work until you succeed.

There will be no time to worry when you are too busy taking constant action.

Always have the belief in your heart and soul that you will succeed.
Never let a grain of doubt cast a shadow in your eventual path to victory.

Focus is key to all.
What you focus on, you will create.
Worrying is worse than useless,
it is DETRIMENTAL to your future.

Take control of your thoughts.
When worry pops its ugly head, force it out with a positive thought of your future.
Don't let the negative illusions of worry live rent-free in your mind.

You are in control here.
Of what you watch,
What you read,
What you listen too
And what you think.

What you think of consistently will become.
Focus on what you want, and how to get there is crucial for lasting happiness and success.

# Chapter 25:

# How to Stop Chasing New Goals All the Time

The philosopher Alan Watts always said that life is like a song, and the sole purpose of the song is to dance. He said that when we listen to a song, we don't dance to get to the end of the music. We dance to enjoy it. This isn't always how we live our lives. Instead, we rush through our moments, thinking there's always something better, there's always some goal we need to achieve.

**"Existence is meant to be fun. It doesn't go anywhere; it just is."**
Our lives are not about things and status. Even though we've made ourselves miserable with wanting, we already have everything we need. Life is meant to be lived. If you can't quit your job tomorrow, enjoy where you are. Focus on the best parts of every day. Believe that everything you do has a purpose and a place in the world.

Happiness comes from gratitude. You're alive, you have people to miss when you go to work, and you get to see them smile every day. We all have to do things we don't want to do; we have to survive. When you find yourself working for things that don't matter, like a big house or a fancy car, when you could be living, you've missed the point. You're playing the song, but you're not dancing.

**"A song isn't just the ending. It's not just the goal of finishing the song. The song is an experience."**

We all think that everything should be amazing when we're at the top, but it's not. Your children have grown older, and you don't remember the little things.

**"…tomorrow and plans for tomorrow can have no significance at all unless you are in full contact with the reality of the present since it is in the present and only in the present that you live."**

You feel cheated of your time, cheated by time. Now you have to make up for it. You have to live, make the most of what you have left. So you set another goal.

This time you'll build memories and see places, do things you never got the chance to do. The list grows, and you wonder how you'll get it all done and still make your large mortgage payment. You work more hours so you can do all this stuff "someday." You've overwhelmed yourself again.

You're missing the point.

Stop wanting more, be grateful for today. Live in the moment. Cherish your life and the time you have in this world. If it happens, it happens. If it doesn't, then it wasn't meant to; let it go.

**"We think if we don't interfere, it won't happen."**

There's always an expectation, always something that has to get done. You pushed aside living so that you could live up to an expectation that doesn't exist to anyone but you. The expectation is always there because you gave it power. To live, you've got to let it go.

You save all your money so that you can retire. You live to retire. Then you get old, and you're too tired to live up to the expectation you had of retirement; you never realize your dreams.

At forty, you felt cheated; at eighty, you are cheated. You cheated yourself the whole way through to the end.

**"Your purpose was to dance until the end, but you were so focused on the end that you forgot to dance."**

# Chapter 26:

# Six Ways To Stop Procrastinating

## Why Procrastinate?

There are a million reasons why you should postpone what you intend to do. Procrastination can come in many ways, most of which are very attractive. Its repercussions are severe and unforgiving. You could miss out on once-in-a-lifetime opportunities, and you will have no one to blame but yourself.

It's not a surprise that you may have unsuccessfully tried to stop procrastinating. Here are tried, tested, and proven six ways how you can overcome it:

## 1. Be Decisive

Your indecisiveness is the reason why you always postpone your scheduled activities. Purpose to be proactive. When you think about doing something, act immediately. Do not shelf any plans you may have for whatever reason no matter how genuine it may look. There is never an opportune time to act.

If you may require resources to implement your plan, move towards getting them instead of waiting for someone else. Try to be self-dependent instead of relying much on other people's help.

However, you will have to operate on other people's schedules if you always depend on them. Get things done yourself and help shall find you halfway.

## 2. Think Out Aloud

This is effective especially for very forgetful people. They procrastinate even in the few times they remember. An important lesson is that there is never a next time.

Instead of making mental notes about what you plan to do, say it aloud. You are likely to remember what you said aloud more than what was in your mind. Keep reminding yourself by saying aloud (not too loud) what you want to do shortly.

This is helpful especially if you are alone. Constantly repeating the same thing can be a nuisance to the people you are with. Here is another way if you are not alone.

## 3. Enlist Your Friends' Help

If your plans are neither sensitive nor personal, you can ask the next person to remind you. Your involvement with other people will have them put you in check.

They will act as prefects over you. Since procrastination is a choice to postpone an act, having a second person who knows what you are supposed to do will enforce personal accountability. You are more likely to ignore what you enlisted to do alone than when someone else is 'monitoring' you.

## 4. Fix Yourself First

You could be blaming your procrastination on other things when you are the problem. You can hardly see the problem within yourself. As much as there could be other causes of procrastination, do a self-audit of yourself.

Are you lacking the psyche to do anything? If you literally need to be pushed even if there is an urgency for you to act, then you are the problem.

Read motivational literature on personal development to lift your spirit. You can also talk to people who will inspire you to action. Motivated people do not procrastinate.

## 5. Fix Your Attitude Towards Work

Regardless of the level of your motivation, you will procrastinate if you have a bad attitude towards work. Check on your attitude towards what you often procrastinate about.

Do you love what you do or you would rather be doing something else? Have a good attitude towards everything you do and you will have the motivation to do what it is.

You can know your attitude through your thoughts. If you have bad thoughts about an act, you will always procrastinate when it comes to implementing it. A good attitude will make you swift in your action.

## 6. Plan Ahead

While the problem could not be about lacking a good plan, it is important to check on your plans if you want to stop procrastination.

Group similar activities together and implement them to completion before starting other tasks. It is easier to complete tasks when you cluster them together based on their characteristics.

For example, labor-intensive work should be done together. Mental tasks should be grouped to be done together too.

These six ways will help you be prompt in your actions and stop procrastination.

# Chapter 27:

# Stay Focused

A razor-sharp focus is required to bridge the gap
between our vision and our current circumstances.
Stay focused on the vision we want,
despite the current reality.
It's challenging to believe you will be rich when you are poor,
healthy if you are sick,
but it is necessary to achieve that vision.

Focus on the desired result.
Focus on the next step towards that goal.
Without focus on these elements there can be no success.
Stay focused on the positive elements,
solutions over problems.

The expected reward over the fear, loss and pain along the way.
What we focus on will become.
Therefore we have to maintain our eyes on the prize.

Be results driven.
Always focus on bringing that result closer.
Focus on what your grateful for.

Gratefulness brings more of that into your life.
Focus on problems on the other hand brings more problems.

If we focus on a big goal today,
we might not be ready yet,
but we will become ready on the way.

Commit to the necessary changes you know you need.
Get ourselves ready for that goal.
So many never act simply because they don't know how.
They don't feel ready.
We can achieve nearly anything if we focus on it.

Think carefully about what you focus on.
It is critical to both your success and failure.
Know exactly what you want.
See the odds of a successful happy life increase by unfathomable amounts.

How can we be happy and successful if we never define what that is?
It's not about what you are, or what you were in the past.
It is all about what you are becoming and want to become.

We cannot let circumstances, or the world decide that.
We must use our free will and decide who and what we will become and focus fully on that.
Wishing, succumbing to the day's whim, will never bring lasting success.

Success requires serious commitment and focus on that outcome.
Exude a fanatical level of focus.
Be exuberated in the pursuit of success.

The most successful often focus on work for over 100 hours per week.
They give up most social interaction and even sleep to make that dream happen.
They do not find this hard or stressful because they are pursuing something they enjoy.

Focus on something you enjoy.
Stop spending your time and energy on a job that you hate.
Work in an area you enjoy.
It makes focusing and achieving success easier.

Keep in mind that your time is limited.
Is what you're doing right now moving you towards your goal?
If not stop.

It is crucial that you enjoy your journey.
Start planning some leisure time into your days.
The goal is to remain balanced while you stick to your schedule.

If you focus on nothing, you will receive nothing.
If you do nothing, you will become nothing.

Your focus is everything.

Get specific with your focus to steer your ships in the direction of the solid fertile land you desire.

Aim higher as you focus on bigger and better things.

Why focus on plan b if you believe in plan a?

Why not give all your focus to that?

Stay focused on the best result regardless of the perceived situation.

The world is pliable.

It will mold and change around you based on your thoughts and what you focus on.

Your free will means you are free to focus on what you want and ignore what you don't.

Focus on a future of greatness.

A future where you are healthy, happy, and wealthy.

See the limits as imaginary and watch them break down before you.

Understand that you are powerful and what you think matters in your life.

Become who you want to be,

Not who others think you should be.

This shift is one of the quickest roads to happiness.

When you focus on what you love,

You draw more of it into our lives.

You will become happier.

You must focus on a future that makes you and your family happy.

You must stay steadfast with an unwavering faith and focus on that result.

Because with faith and focus anything is possible.

# Chapter 28:

# Focus - The Art of Alignment

Focus. A buzzword in the workspace. Everyone wants to have focus and keep focus. If you want it, you got to understand it. Focus is not some abstract notion that comes and goes as it pleases. It only seems like that because you haven't learnt the rhythm of focus. Do you know what lures it in? Do you know what keeps it there once it comes?

Because at its core, focus is quite simple. If we look at a laser, we see a focused beam of light, how? Lasers are concentrated light waves, in order for it to work the waves have to be coming from the same base, be going in the same direction, and be almost perfectly in sync.

Let me tell you that if you need to know who you are and what you want, because otherwise nothing will be coming from the same base. Everything that you do should stem from knowing who you are and who you want to be. If you know those two things then you start to bring everything into that bigger picture, you start every activity from that foundation.

If you want to be a professional athlete, then you go to your office job knowing that this is just a means to support your training and future career. You know that the better you perform there the closer you become to financial freedom and the more you can invest time into the thing you want to become. Not only will that motivate you to push through the mundane, but you will find constant fulfilment because everything you do will seem to bring you closer to your goals. Even if they are not related at all. If you are looking to become the CEO of a big company, then you take the time to focus on cleaning your house because you cannot expect to bring order outside of your home if you do not have control within it.

Your first step to focus is finding your base and your direction, knowing who you are and who you want to be. Then you bring everything in sync with that. Because when everything flows in the patterns of your passion, focus is inevitable.

What about a camera? They focus by shifting the lens towards and away from the film. This means the light converges before or directly on the film, or it doesn't get to converge at all. When light converges all the points of it line up in a way that produces a clear picture. The art of photography is finding positioning it in such a way that what you want to capture is focused. If you want to capture first place, if you want to get that promotion, whatever you want to do. You need to be able to adjust your focus so that the things you want are clear, and everything else blurs slightly into the background. Blurring does not distort your vision, it brings clarity to the primary focus. It ensures the desirable image of the future is sharp which means allowing the obstacles to blur into the process. When your focus is right, you don't get tempted by distractions. You see the bigger picture in light of your goals, not the deviations from them.

# Chapter 29:

# Hitting Rock Bottom

Today we're going to talk about a topic that I hope none of you will have to experience at any point in your lives. It can be a devastating and painful experience and I don't wish it on my worst enemy, but if this happens to be you, I hope that in today's video I can help you get out of the depths and into the light again.

First of all, I'm not going to waste any more time but just tell you that hitting rock bottom could be your blessing in disguise. You see when we hit rock bottom, the only reason that we know we are there is because we have become aware and have admitted to ourselves that there is no way lower that we can go. That we know deep in our hearts that things just cannot get any worse than this. And that revelation can be enlightening. Enlightening in the sense that by simple law of physics, the worse that can happen moving forward is either you move sideways, or up. When you have nothing more left to lose, you can be free to try and do everything in your power to get back up again.

For a lot of us who have led pretty comfortable lives, sometimes it feels like we are living in a bubble. We end up drifting through life on the comforts of our merits that we fail to stop learning and growing as people. We become so jaded about everything that life becomes bland.

We stop trying to be better, we stop trying to care, and we that in itself could be poison. It is like a frog getting boiled gradually, we don't notice it until it is too late, and we are cooked. We are in fact slowly dying and fading into irrelevance.

But when you are at rock bottom, you become painfully aware of everything. Painfully aware of maybe your failed relationships, the things you did and maybe the people you hurt that have led you to this point. You become aware that you need to change yourself first, that everything starts with growing and learning again from scratch, like a baby learning how to walk again. And that could be a very rewarding time in your life when you become virtually fearless to try and do anything in your power to get back on your feet again.

Of course, all this has to come from you. That you have to make the decision that things will never stay the same again. That you will learn from your mistakes and do the right things. When you've hit rock bottom, you can slowly begin the climb one step at a time.

Start by defining the first and most important thing that you cannot live without in life. If family means the most to you, reach out to them. Find comfort and shelter in them and see if they are able to provide you with any sort of assistance while you work on your life again. I always believe that if family is the most important thing, and that people you call family will be there with you till the very end. If family is not available to you, make it a priority to start growing a family. Family doesn't mean you have to have blood relations. Family is whoever you can rely on in your darkest times. Family is people who will accept you and love you for who you are in spite of your shortcomings. Family is people that will help nurture and get you back on your own two feet again. If you don't have family, go get one.

If hitting rock bottom to you means that you feel lost in life, in your career and finance, that you may be lost your businesses and are dealing with the aftermath, maybe your first priority is to simply find a simple part time job that can occupy your time and keep you sustained while you figure out what to do next. Sometimes all we need is a little break to clear our heads and to start afresh again. Nothing ever stays the same. Things will get better. But don't fall into the trap of ruminating on your losses as it can be very destructive on your mental health. The past has already happened, and you cannot take it back. Take stock of the reasons and don't make the same mistakes again in your career and you will be absolutely fine.

If you feel like you've hit rock bottom because of a failed marriage or relationship, whether it be something you did or your partner did, I know this can be incredibly painful and it feels like you've spent all your time with someone with nothing to show for it but wasted time and energy but know that things like that happen and that it is perfectly normal. Humans are flawed and we all make mistakes. So yes, it is okay to morn over the loss of the relationship and feel like you can't sink any lower, but don't lose faith as you will find someone again.

If hitting rock bottom is the result of you being ostracized by people around you for not being a good person, where you maybe have lost all the relationships in your life because of something you did, I'm sure you know the first step to do is to accept that you need to change. Don't look to someone else to blame but look inwards instead. Find time where you can go away on your way to reflect on what went wrong. Start going through the things that people were unhappy with you about and start looking for ways to improve yourself. If you need help, I am here for you. If not, maybe you might want to seek some professional help as well to dig a little deeper and to help guide you along a better path.

Hitting rock bottom is not a fun thing, and I don't want to claim that I know every nuance and feeling of what it means to get there, but I did feel like that once when my business failed on me, and I made the decision that I could only go up from here. I started to pour all my time and energy into proving to myself that I will succeed no matter what and that I will not sit idly by and feel sorry for myself. It was a quite a journey, but I came out of it stronger than before and realized that I was more resourceful than I originally thought.

So I challenge each and every one of you who feels like you've hit the bottom to not be afraid of taking action once again. To be fearless and just take that next right step forward no matter what. And I hope to see you on the top of the mountain in time to come.

# Chapter 30:

# Positive Thinking For Men

Positive thinking is not a boon that is bestowed only to the gurus who teach the art of living. It is at everyone's disposal. With seeds of cynicism easily growing in the minds of men, positive thinking is the only anchor that one can hold on to.

Here are some steps to help you become a positive thinker.

## 1. Control Your Attitude

Sometimes the conscious decision not to think negatively and to conquer the negativity around you helps in shaping your outlook towards life. People often end up making the mistake of letting others or certain situations dictate the terms of their life. You should try and avoid this at all costs and try to make these crucial decisions yourself.

## 2. Meditate

The ascetics of bygone times have meditated for centuries to attain nirvana. Meditation, thus, has been an age-old ruse to connect with oneself. Scientists believe that during meditation, when the mind focuses on a particular stream of thought, it starts radiating a certain kind of energy. This energy can empower individuals to take on the hurdles in life and eventually overcome them. Try and meditate for 10 minutes every day. Pick a dark room away from distractions, close your eyes and breathe deeply. Try to clear your mind of all thoughts. This might seem difficult at the start, but with practice, it will become much easier.

## 3. Meet Positive People

Every person in this world has something to offer to the larger collective thought process. Meeting positive people keeps your thoughts and goals heading towards a positive direction, while negative people pull out all positive energy from your life. Try to seek the company of people who give out positive vibes. You will certainly <u>feel the difference</u> in yourself.

## 4. Stand by Your Goals

Set your goal in accordance with your heartfelt ambitions. Stand by them no matter how impossible they might seem. Start believing in them and work towards achieving them. The world has numerous fresh perspectives to offer and with an open and optimistic mind, adopting such fresh perspectives will change your life for the better. Work hard and step closer to reaching your goals. Once you have achieved them, you will be inspired to take on newer adventures. With each goal achieved, no matter how small, you will feel empowered and confident of your abilities.

## 5. Change Your Mental Build

How you react to certain situations in life ends up making a difference in your overall thinking abilities. Maintaining a positive reaction to hardships makes the difficult periods seem bearable and easy to sail through, whereas negative thought processes only make hardships seem bigger than they actually are. A change in your outlook will let you see the world with a new perspective, and you might see beauty in life that you never thought existed.

## 6. Question Your Behaviour

It is the natural characteristic of a man, to resist any sort of change. But when you turn around and questions your own motive for resistance, you end up seeing a problem as much smaller than what was previously anticipated. Thus, questioning your motives diminishes your defensive nature and helps you remain open to possibilities for more experience.

# 5. Choose Your Words Carefully

One habit that is essential to positive thinking is to transform your vocabulary. The words you choose – both in conversation and in your own mind – have a deep impact on your mindset. Studies have found that positive self-talk improves psychological states, helps people regulate their emotions and more. Your conversation affects how others respond to you, again creating a feedback loop that can be either positive or negative.

Before you can choose different words, you need to recognize what words you're already using. Take note of how you label and describe things in conversation, particularly your own emotions. Are you really "terrified" of that big work presentation or just a little nervous? Are you truly "angry" at your partner or mildly annoyed at one of their bad habits? When you dial back your vocabulary and use words that are less emotionally loaded, you'll find your mindset becomes attuned to more positive thinking.

Many people find it helpful to write down negative words they find themselves using throughout the day. For every negative word, write a positive alternative next to it. Keep the alternatives in the back of your mind to use next time. Find this aspect of positive thinking overwhelming? Start with just one area of your life that causes negative thoughts, like work or your relationship status. Catch yourself in those moments, and build from there.

You should remember that positivity attracts positivity and negativity only attracts negativity. Thus, by thinking positively, you are opening yourself to a host of new possibilities and experiences and are thus making your <u>life worth living</u>.